ALISON LAYT

Life Lessons with Theodore

A 12 step reflective journal towards embracing life

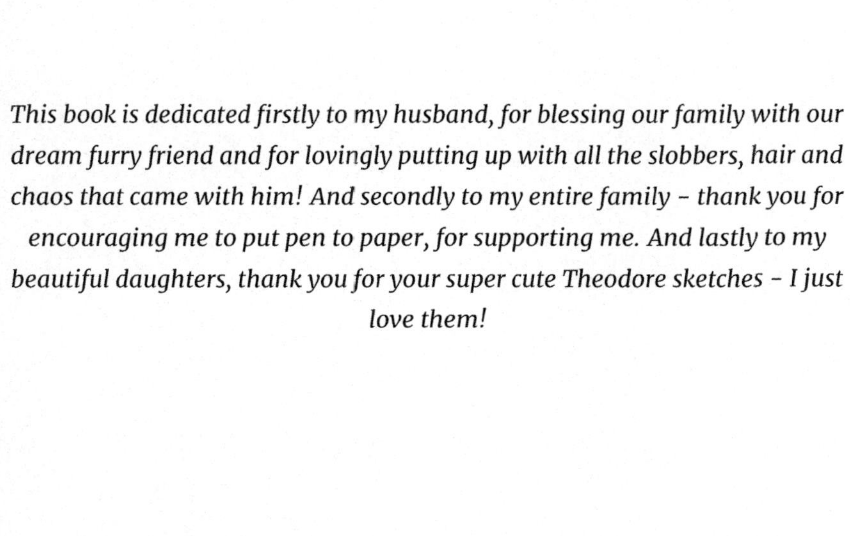

This book is dedicated firstly to my husband, for blessing our family with our dream furry friend and for lovingly putting up with all the slobbers, hair and chaos that came with him! And secondly to my entire family – thank you for encouraging me to put pen to paper, for supporting me. And lastly to my beautiful daughters, thank you for your super cute Theodore sketches – I just love them!

Contents

Introduction

It is often said that a dog is "man's best friend". Over the years of my life, I have seen this to be true. True for me, and true for my family. When you are sad, they bring joy; when you are tired, they bring energy; when you are lonely, they're your always and ever companion; and when you want something to snuggle, they are up for the hug!

Our giant, big, doofus of a slobbery dog Theodore was our bestie. The joy he brought, his hilarious antics, his ridiculously stubborn personality all made life such an absolute blast. He left hair and slobber everywhere he went - in the car, on our clothes, in the house, on the walls, on the floor, even on the ceiling! Yes - everywhere! I can hear you saying, "That is so gross!" and it totally was gross, but we would not have changed it for the world! He brought a whole lot of joy, laughter, and love.

You can probably tell by the way that I am writing that he is no longer with us. He lived a life way too short for our liking, not quite making his third birthday. We found out the week we were to collect him that he had a heart condition. We decided that regardless of his medical concerns, he needed a family and he needed love. We already loved him so it was a no brainer for us to bring him home to be a part of our big family. My husband and I are blessed to have five beautiful children; one is married, so now we have six young adult children. From the moment we met Theodore our family were madly in love. From the get-go he was a character - playful but stubborn, mischievous, and snuggly. He taught our family so much and brought us closer together.

Theodore and I spent a lot of time together. I loved to walk; he loved to walk. I loved the beach; he loved the beach. That made him my perfect beach walking partner. More often than not, I would ponder life on our walks due to something Theodore would do (or something that he would not do!). And that is how this collection of short stories and reflections evolved. This book is a compilation of some of my ponderings; a kind of journal I suppose. My short time with Theodore encouraged and challenged me in so many areas of my life, in ways that brought the best out of me. I'd love to share these thoughts with you in the hope that they encourage you to live out your very best life.

We've all been given this precious gift of life. We have no idea how long our journey will be here on earth, but one thing is certain - I want to enjoy my life. I want to look to the possibilities rather than the impossibilities and go for it. I want to embrace life, to live this adventure with all that I am and with my favourite people right by my side. Just like my big beastie and bestie, Theodore. If this sounds like something you want to do, then join me on this journey. Come with me and see what you too can learn from my best furry friend.

This journal can be read from front to back very quickly over a few cups of tea. The stories and reflections are short and to the point, so they're perfect for a lazy, rainy, kind of day. You could simply skim over the questions and challenges and see what, if anything, stands out to you.

Or, the book can be read slowly, one story at a time. Perhaps a reflection a week, taking you on a twelve-week journey. By reading it in this way, you'll have time to ponder the questions and lessons that are in it for you and decide what actions you would like to take. There is no right or wrong way to read and use this journal. The fact that you have picked it up and read it this far puts a huge smile on my face.

I hope you enjoy these reflections. I hope that I have done my gorgeous Theodore justice in my stories. I hope that it encourages you, even just a little, to embrace the life that you've been given. If it does, let me know! I'd love to hear your insights if you'd like to share your story with me.

Enjoy getting to know my big, hairy, slobbery giant. He'll live in my family's hearts forever and I hope these lessons will too.

Aly Layt xx

Chasing Tails to Chasing Dreams

"Chase your dreams. Don't wait till the dreams come true."
Greyson Chance

Have you ever found yourself going round and round in circles – like my crazy dog?

Today at the beach the water was crystal clear. It was calm. The tide was high, so Theodore was loving his swim. He had the whole beach to himself. So what did he do? He opted to swim around in circles, chasing his tail! He could be swimming after the fish or chasing me, but no! He used up his energy chasing his tail.And he didn't go anywhere!

Have you ever done this? Have you ever found yourself going around in circles? Working hard but not getting anywhere? Using up all your energy yet not going where you need to go or getting done what you need to get done? I have. Many times. This particular moment is a standout for me though....

I remember being in a season quite some time ago now where I was working full time as a Year Two teacher. I had five young children, a husband working twelve-hour days, and we were renovating our home.

It truly was nuts with all seven of us humans and our two dogs living in a tiny house – on what seemed to be more-or-less a work site! The kids played soccer (hubby coached) and I volunteered in our local church. I remember feeling a bit overwhelmed and down and simply wanting some "me" time along with desperately wanting to find some time to exercise. I kept going around and around, doing what needed to be done but I could not find a way to find the time for me or for exercise.

One day I distinctly remember thinking *"enough is enough"*! I was so tired of going around in circles! Sure, I didn't have time for a decent walk, but I realised I could spare five minutes! There and then I quit thinking about it, and decided that I would go for a walk around the block. And that is what I did. I quickly threw on some shoes and walked around the block. From that point on in my life I stopped chasing my tail (unlike my Theodore) to making the changes in my life I desired. I went from wishing and hoping for more time, to walking around the block. That short, five-minute walk has grown dramatically over the years. I began to walk, then run daily, growing from five minutes, to eventually five kilometres, to years later having run trail and road marathons, to most recently completing my first 100km ultra marathon! I found time to walk at crazy hours of the day with friends, to go to the gym and participate in bootcamps, meeting many amazing people along the way. All because one day, when I thought I had absolutely no time to spare, I quit going round and around and intentionally did **one** thing. I walked around the block.

My challenge: Are you going around in circles chasing your tail? What do you *really* want? What is one thing that you can change right now, today? Do it now! Don't overthink it, your future self will be ever so thankful.

* * *

Going Deeper...

In what ways are you going around and around in circles? This could be in your relationships, especially your intimate relationship, in your family life, in your workplace, in your career, your health, emotions, or perhaps your finances?

Is it working for you to continue going around in that circle? What will happen if nothing changes?

What do you want to do instead? Even if it doesn't seem possible? Be specific.

What is one thing that you can do differently today that can break the endless cycle of going around and around? The one small change that can break you out of survival mode and move you into living intentionally? What is one small change that you can make today, that can begin your journey towards the lifestyle that so far you have only dreamt of? Write it down and decide to do it today!

Distraction – The Thief of our Desires

"Don't be on your deathbed someday, having squandered your one chance at life, full of regret because you pursued little distractions instead of big dreams."
Derek Sivers

This morning I was attempting to walk home with Theodore after a swim at the beach. The problem was, Theo didn't want to go home. So, what did he do? He planted himself firmly down, facing the direction he wanted to go, which was back towards the beach. Now as you can probably imagine this was quite the hilarious sight for onlookers. Both of us parked on the footpath. Both standing our ground. Theodore facing the beach and me coaxing him in the opposite direction. His body weight is approximately the same, if not a touch more than mine. I wasn't sure I was going to win this battle!

Theodore sat firmly and faced exactly where he wanted to go, with his eyes focused on the beach. The beach was his one desire, his one goal. Luckily for me Theodore didn't realise his size and power because he could have easily dragged me towards the beach if he had wanted to! So how was I going to get Theodore to turn around and compliantly walk home with me? Instantly, I knew what I needed to do. I needed to distract him. I realised that if I could get Theodore's eyes off the beach, I would be able to get him to walk home with me. I was still left with the problem of how to distract Theodore. My first strategy was boredom. We literally sat there. It felt like a long time, but it was only a few minutes. After boredom, I tried circling him, a technique I had once seen on a dog training show. I would walk a step in the direction he wanted to go, only to circle back to the direction I wanted him to go. After several attempts this finally worked. Tired of sitting in the same spot, Theodore became excited by the movement, and he lost sight of the beach. Once again, he was happy to walk with me. Let me tell you I breathed a huge sigh of relief that this battle was finally over, and I had won!

As I continued my way home it came to my attention that there were many lessons that I could learn from this experience. Here is what I was reminded of:

- When I have a goal that I am working towards, just as Theodore did, I need to sit with it. I need to position my body in the direction I want to go, so I can clearly see where I am headed and firmly fix my eyes on it! I have a number of goals that I am currently working towards. When I am focused, I am determined, excited, passionate, and creative and I take the steps I need to move towards that goal. These are all incredibly important if I want to achieve my goals!

- What causes me to lose sight of my goals? Distraction! Isn't it true that the moment I become distracted from my goals I lose heart, getting caught up in the everyday things and forgetting what I am working towards? I go back to the daily ins and outs of life only to realise at some point down the track that I am no longer heading in the direction I set out towards.

As I walked home, I considered my goals and the power of distraction. I wondered what was distracting me from my goals and causing me to lose sight of them. Was it boredom? Boredom often sneaks in when there is a delay in reaching goals. It is easy to lose sight of my goals or to lose heart when it seems like it is taking forever to get anywhere. Boredom and delay can cause me to forget my passion and the excitement that I once had to go after the things I desire.

Or I wondered if perhaps I am stepping forward in the direction of where I want to go, only to veer slightly off track due to becoming distracted by all the daily happenings in life? Either way, I have realised distraction is leading me away from where I actually want to go.

My encouragement: Sit tight and position your body facing where you want to go. Fix your eyes on your goals. Be determined. Don't allow distraction to cause you to lose sight of where you want to go!

* * *

Going deeper....

What are your goals? If you don't have any, I encourage you to take some time to explore what you really want - for you, your family, your health, career, and finances - in fact, for all that you want to be.

Is your body positioned facing your goals? Can you see where you want to go or where you want to be? You don't need to know how you are going to get there just yet, that comes with taking action. Position yourself to see what you want. What can you see?

Are you taking action towards your goal? If you are, then what steps are you taking? Are those actions effective in creating progress? If not, what could you do differently? What else could you try?

What, if anything, is distracting you? What can you do about it?

What has the potential to distract you? Is there anything that you can you put in place to avoid that trap?

How can you reignite the passion and excitement needed keep you pressing on towards your goals?

Who can you share your goals with to help you to be accountable to yourself on this journey? Or if you can't share with someone, where can you write your goals so that you remember them on the days you find yourself a little distracted?

Living in the Deep

"A ship in the harbour is safe, but that's not what ships are built for."
John A Shedd

Today Theodore went out in search of deep waters. He loves the beach the most when the tide is high, and the water is deep enough to swim. What he doesn't love so much is when the waves crash over his head! But he must think it's worth the risk because he goes out into the deep whenever he can. He always seems just a little disappointed on the days the tide is out, like it is today. He just kept on walking out hoping to find water deep enough to swim, but at the same time he didn't want to stray too far away from me (he's such a mummy's boy).

As I watched Theodore, I realised that all too often we can be the complete opposite to him, tending to avoid the deep waters of life. We prefer to stay where it is "safe", "predictable", with no risk of the "waves crashing over our head". Living within our comfort zone is something that all too often we strive for, but the reality is, there is no growth there!

I wondered what area of my life I needed to go a little deeper in this week. Where perhaps I need to actually kick my legs and paddle to keep my head above the water? I know that we can't live in the deep continuously because we'll likely get tired and wear ourselves out. For me though, I've realised it's where the excitement is. It's a place not only of challenge, but also of growth and freedom.

I think it is important to remember that there are seasons for all things. Perhaps you are in need of a more restful season? There are times for embracing feelings of comfort and safety in our every day. Sometimes we are simply exhausted from madly "paddling our legs" from living in the deep and we need to rest! But perhaps like me, you've realised today that you need to step outside of your comfort zone, and to go a little deeper. I wonder what growth could come for you?

My challenge: Stepping out of our comfort zone can be scary, uncom-fortable, with risks involved, but it can lead to greater growth, freedom, and fulfillment. Are you living within your comfort zone? Are you happy in this space? Or are you feeling down about life, wondering if there is more? Are you up for a challenge to intentionally grow and be all that you've been created to be?

* * *

Going deeper....

What areas of your life are you living too safely? Too close to the shoreline?

What steps could you take that will create further growth in your life? This could be in your business, career, finances, or your relationships.

What growth could occur if you took those steps?

Are there any risks in taking those steps?

Are there areas in your life where you are well and truly in over your head, and you are beginning to tire? What areas are they?

If you are feeling a little worn out from living in the deep, what steps can you take that will enable you to either keep on going or to find time to rest?

Do you need to better resource yourself in this area? Are there books, courses, podcasts, or people in your world that can assist you on your journey? If so, are you using them? If not, what do you need to do?

What's Around the Corner?

Tom Hiddleston

Theodore was living the dream this morning. He'd had a run along the beach, played with some doggy friends and had a swim, so I thought that it was about time to head home. I sensed that he still had a lot of energy to burn and since I didn't want the stalemate mentioned in the earlier chapter, I decided to walk the long way home. Theo had never walked that way before, and he was having a wonderful time sniffing at all the unfamiliar light posts, trees and fences. He was creating quite the scene as we walked by all the houses with dogs barking at us from behind their fences. He loved the chaos of all the barking, causing him to prance along the road, tail held high as we walked. That was until we got approximately one street away from home. At this point Theodore had decided he'd had enough walking and wanted to go home. So, he sat himself down on the road and faced back in the direction that we had come from. He knew that if we walked back that way, that he'd end up where he wanted to be. He had absolutely no clue that just around the corner was in fact exactly where he wanted to be – home!

Theodore was tired of his adventure; he'd had enough and wanted to go home. He was no longer interested in the journey, it was no longer exciting, he'd lost his enthusiasm, and he was worn out.

I wonder if as you read this little story, you - like me - can relate? Are you feeling tired and worn out from this adventure called life? Are you weary from the unfamiliar situations and circumstances that you experience as you go after your goals and dreams? Are you considering turning back to what is the more familiar territory? After all, you know what that journey entails.

My encouragement: I wonder what is around the corner should you stick with the path you're on? Perhaps your destination is not too far away, perhaps it is just around the bend? And perhaps it requires a little courage, some strength, some grit and determination to continue along on the unknown path ... for just a little longer.

* * *

Going deeper....

What life journey are you on? Where are you headed?

Have you lost your sense of adventure and enthusiasm that you need for your life's journey?

I wonder what this means for you? Does it mean you should turn around? If you did, what could you miss out on?

Is there a way to stir up the excitement you once had for the journey? If so, what could that look like?

If your destination was potentially around the corner, what would that do for you?

If you could summon the courage to stick with the path, what will that give you? Where could you end up?

Could it all be worth it?

Variety - the Spice of Life

"Variety's the very spice of life, that gives it all its flavour."
William Cowper

My walks with Theodore typically consist of a similar routine. We walk in the direction towards the beach, we take one of a handful of possible pathways down towards the water so Theo can go for a swim. Today though, as we started walking, it started to rain, ever so lightly. Before long, the sky opened up, and the rain bucketed down! We were completely wet through, so I assumed he would not need a swim. I decided to walk in a different direction, to explore somewhere new. At first Theodore did not agree with my decision at all! He hesitated and attempted to pull in the usual direction. Eventually though, after lots of encouragement, Theo allowed me to lead him in the new direction, to try something new.

Well, it wasn't too long into our walk that Theo fully embraced this new path. There were puddles to play in, new smells to chase after, different trees to lift his leg against and claim as his own! This really opened my eyes to see and reminded me of the importance of trying something new.I realised again that it often requires great intentionality when we want to try something new in our life or when we want to break old habits or patterns. If we want to take a different direction or if we desire to do something fresh and new, it will seem a little weird initially, perhaps even slightly uncomfortable, but there are likely great rewards if we persevere! By adding some variety, old patterns can be broken and replaced with greater opportunities, greater experiences, and greater excitement.

My challenge: I wonder what pattern or habit in our life needs to be slightly tweaked, or completely overhauled? I wonder what new experiences will be presented when we add some variety to our world?

* * *

Going deeper....

What habits or patterns are in your life?

Is it serving you well to do the same thing, the same way, time and time again?

What are some patterns or habits you have in your life that you would like to change?

Could adding variety to your routine create room for that change? Could you replace your old habit with a new experience?

What could that look like?

How could that change your life?

The need for variety is one of our core needs as humans. How important is the need for variety in your life?

Channelling My Inner Theodore

"The most beautiful thing you can wear is confidence."
Blake Lively

I can't help but notice how my dog walks down the street. He has this prance. A very playful yet confident stride. He holds his fluffy tail high and somehow the expression on his face is a mixture of goofiness and pride all at once! I can't help but smile at the way he greets other dogs on his walk. He stares in their direction, making eye contact the entire time as they walk towards him and then he stops to stay hello as they approach. Theodore assumes that any dog walking in his direction must want to stop and say hello to him, to sniff him and have a quick play.

This made me chuckle as I imagined myself doing the same. Firstly, I imagined myself prancing into a room filled with strangers and brimming with confidence! But then my pondering turned a little more serious. Imagine if I *was* to walk into a room of unfamiliar faces and simply assume that they wanted to say hello and connect with me? Imagine if I thought they would be interested in talking with me and getting to know me and what I do? Wouldn't that cause me to walk into such a room with greater confidence? To walk as though I belong? I wonder what difference this could make in my life? So, if you see me prancing along, with a fun loving, goofy expression on my face as I enter a room – know I am embracing my inner Theodore!!

Now I am fully aware that this could perhaps come across as arrogance, but there is a big difference between arrogance and confidence! Arrogance is to look down on others and to consider ourselves as better than they are. Confidence is simply believing in ourselves, and that we belong. Walking with confidence is attractive, it draws people to each other. It is a beautiful trait to have, and it has the potential to bring out the very best in us!

My encouragement: Pay attention to your body language. How do you stand when you walk into a space that is unfamiliar? How do you walk into a room filled with people you don't know? How do you feel? What are you saying to yourself? Could you and should you channel your inner Theodore?

* * *

Going deeper....

On a scale from 1 to 10 - with 10 walking like Theodore and 1 being at the opposite end, with a complete lack of confidence - where are you?

How is that working for you? Do you want to improve your level of confidence?

What problems, if any, are created by your lack of confidence?

What is holding you back from being more confident? Is it a belief about yourself?

How could you change your body language to instill more confidence? Could you stand tall? Give eye contact? Be specific.

What about your self-talk? How do you normally talk to yourself in situations where you know you are lacking confidence?

What could you say to yourself that could increase your confidence? Plan for an occasion to put this into practice!

The Gift of Eye Contact

"The eyes are the window to the soul."
William Shakespeare

When Theodore looks at us, it's like his eyes truly see deep into our soul. It's not just me that experiences this, but the whole family. I'm not entirely sure what it is that causes us to feel like that. Perhaps it's the sheer size of him and his eyes, or their colour, or the intensity that seems to be behind his gaze. One thing that I know for sure, Theodore shows his deep love for his family through his eyes and it's so very special for us on the receiving end.

This got me thinking about the gift of eye contact and how powerfully special it is. Many years ago, in my final year of high school, before my now hubby (Aaron) and I were dating, I became very aware of this powerful form of communication. Towards the end of the school year, most of the Year 12 students would gather around picnic tables during lunchtime (a place we fondly called "the beer garden") and play cards. Aaron and I were part of the same friendship group, but one day I noticed something. As I got up to leave the card game, I noticed his eyes glance over his hand and our eyes met. And there it was. I knew in an instant that his feelings for me had changed. His eyes had said it all.

Eyes can speak of love, joy, laughter, intense sadness, or of loneliness. They often tell a story and simply catching someone's eyes, with an added smile, can really encourage and make their day. There is such beauty in the eyes. They connect us together and they allow us to truly see one another. One of our core needs as humans is for love and connection. To be seen, known, loved, and understood is so deeply important to all of us. It is so amazing that our eyes have the ability to communicate this, to both show love and connection, and to receive it.

My challenge: The gift of eye contact is just one way of allowing us to connect with people and the world around us. It's a way of bringing us together and joining us to our loved ones. It's a way of communicating, especially when words cannot be used. How is your eye contact? Are you communicating your connection to those who need to know it in your world?

* * *

Going deeper...

Take note over the next few days how often you connect with others through eye contact. What are you noticing? What is being communicated?

When you are out in the world what are you communicating through your eyes to those around you?

Consider your more intimate relationships. How do you connect through your eyes? Do you take time to really see your spouse? Your children?

Do you need to make any changes?

Stir Ourselves Up

Typically speaking, every second Wednesday at 5:30am, Aaron's alarm goes off. At the sound of this noise, Theodore can barely contain his excitement. It means only one thing to him – Road Trip! A trip in the car to the airport to drop Daddy so he can fly off to work for the week. This trip takes approximately 15 minutes. It is also worth noting that this is not his only car trip, but nonetheless it is something that he loves to do. As soon as the alarm goes off, Theodore is at the door. If we let him inside, he is at our feet, watching our every move, trying to maintain eye contact, waiting for us to ask him one of his most favourite questions - "Theodore, do you want to go for a drive?"

The moment this question is delivered, Theodore goes nuts, sprinting around inside the house, up and down the hallway. When we head outside, he runs around like crazy, bounding around the yard. His crazy energy rubs off on us and we all get excited about the drive (well not sure I would say my husband is that excited to be heading off to work for the week!). But we all have a laugh and a big smile on our face, there is excitement in the air, and I am fairly certain the whole street hears all the commotion!

There is something to be said about getting excited about the seemingly ordinary, everyday things. It stirs us up, gives us energy and lights a fire in our belly. It exudes fun and joy, something that can be sadly absent in our every day.

My challenge: How often do you get excited throughout the day? What everyday things do you do that is lacking some fun? If you could add a little extra passion or energy, what could that change?

* * *

Going deeper....

What are some areas in your life that have become mundane and boring. Is there something that you dread doing?

What would happen if you allowed the mundane and the boring to continue without making any changes?

What could you do to make these experiences more enjoyable? Spend some time to come up with several ideas – be creative!

How could you put more energy and joy into the experience?

What difference could that change make to your day?

What difference could it make to the people around you?

Rest and Reset

Today one of my boys hilariously called out "Mum, can we trade Theo in for a real dog?", he was joking of course! Here is what was going on - Theodore was refusing to play with him; in fact, he was ignoring him completely! When Theodore decided he's not doing anything, absolutely nothing can change his mind. We'd call his name and he'd pretend not to hear us. He had been known to walk past us on many occasions as soon as we'd open the front door and let him in the house. Without him even so much as glancing in our direction he would head directly to his bed. No amount of calling his name could cause him to even turn his head towards us! When Theodore was tired, he did one of the things he did best.... sleep. He'd snore the day away until he was refreshed, reset and ready to engage and play once again. Nothing or no one could change his mind!

This is something I really need to learn from my big fluffy beast! I so easily get caught up in the day and all the happenings, regardless of how I am feeling. And if I am exhausted, well too bad, I'd have to just keep going. Now it is important to know that every time we feel tired, we just can't ignore our responsibilities, but if we want to show up in life as the best version of ourselves, then we must take good care of our bodies and rest when needed. Rest and recovery are of vital importance to our health and wellbeing. It brings the best out of us, refreshes us, and helps us to bring more energy and creativity to everything we do. It enables us to balance what is in our hands, yet it is something that so many of us so easily ignore.

My encouragement: When did you last rest and reset? Take a leaf out of Theodore's book, ignore the world, ignore social media, and take a moment to rest!

* * *

Going deeper...

What do you enjoy doing that helps you to relax and recuperate?

How often do you take time for yourself and to rest? Is it often enough?

What barriers are in the way of taking time to rest?

What do you need to do to break through those barriers?

Do you need to schedule time into your week to rest and to look after your body? What could that look like?

What would happen if you ignored the need to rest? If you continued to run on empty?

Help! Dealing with the Unexpected

"When you next find yourself in a state of uncertainty, resist your fear. Shift your focus to where you want to go and your actions will take you in that direction."
Tony Robbins

This morning I was inside the house when Theodore suddenly started barking. And not just his little bark, it was his big, scary, deep bark alerting me that something was wrong. I sprinted outside to see him running up and down the fence between us and our neighbour's house. It is worth pointing out here that there is a gate between our properties and Theodore gets invited over every afternoon for a treat and play with our wonderful neighbours. He has a deep love for the ladies next door and Theo pretty much views both houses as his own territory.

But back to the story. Theo was running like crazy, going up and down the fence with his scary bark. I just stood there trying to figure out what was going on. I looked around. Nothing. I looked for a snake. Still nothing. Then I noticed it. A box. An empty, discarded, cardboard box that my neighbour had left on the grass. Surely that wasn't what was causing all this huge reaction? I tried to calm Theo down. He eventually came and stood by my side, and I explained to him that it was only a box (it's ridiculous how often I try to speak sense to him, after all he is a dog and does not speak English!). After a moment, I opened the gate to let him through to explore this box. Well Theodore barrelled quickly towards that box, with his huge scary bark, only to then step wide and sprint past it, continuing to bark at it. It was hilarious. I couldn't believe it. Theodore was scared of the box. He was scared of an empty, cardboard box! In his mind the box shouldn't have been there, it was unfamiliar, it was out of place, and it was unexpected - therefore it was obviously scary!

There were several other incidents that played out similarly to the above story. Theodore had a scary encounter when the catcher from our mower was left out in the yard and on another occasion, he discovered an upside-down bucket. All equally scary objects I think you would agree?!

As I chuckled over Theodore's reaction, I began to wonder how many times I've been afraid of the unknown, afraid of the unexpected? I wondered how many times I may have overreacted out of fear rather than approaching something with curiosity?

My challenge: When have you been afraid of the unknown? Is that the first emotion that you experience? Have you ever overreacted? Do you need to be afraid?

* * *

Going deeper....

Have you experienced fear of the unknown before? Think of a time that you experienced this fear, what were you afraid of?

Have you overreacted out of fear? What did you do?

Did this overreaction impact you? Or others around you?

Did the unknown end up being as scary as you first thought?

What will you do next time you are in a similar situation?

How can you approach unknown, or unfamiliar situations from now on?

Be a Comfort

"Just being there for someone can sometimes bring hope when all seems hopeless."
David Llewellyn

My daughter Abby came home upset today. As I gave her a hug and she was explaining what was going on in her world, Theodore ran from his bed, going directly to Abby. You could tell by his response that he knew she was upset. He wasn't about to leave her side. This never happens, but Theo slept outside my daughter's bedroom when she went inside (she doesn't let him in with all his hair and slobber!). Once he was comfortable that she was okay, Theodore left her doorway. Dogs are amazing like that aren't they? They are so aware of their human's emotions, their needs. What I really noticed in this time was that even though Theodore's company didn't change any of the circumstances for my daughter, his presence brought some comfort, love, and protection.

How many times have I felt inadequate when my family or friends were going through some difficult situations, because I couldn't do anything, because I couldn't change the circumstances for them? What a beautiful reminder that even though in life there will be hard times that we all must walk through, we can sit with people in that space, and simply being with them can bring comfort, love, and protection. It can be just the encouragement they need to help them to continue to put one foot in front of the other. It doesn't change their circumstances, but it can have the power to change their heart and their experience. I was reminded to never underestimate the power of partnering with people on their journey, sitting with them in that space, being with them and reminding them that they are not alone.

My encouragement: You don't need to have the answers or know what to do to support your loved ones on their life journey... more often than not, you simply need to be there, to love and partner with them, judgement free.

* * *

Going deeper...

What thoughts came to mind as you read through this story?

When has someone partnered with you during difficult times? What did it feel like? How did it help?

Perhaps you haven't experienced being on the receiving end of this kind of partnership. What has prevented this in your life? What can you do about it moving forward?

How can you partner with someone in your world today (or in the future)? What could that look like?

How can you show up for your loved ones judgement free, especially while they are in that vulnerable space?

What is the gift in this partnership?

Embracing Life

"Life is too short, the world is too big and God's love too great to live ordinary."
Christine Caine

This week I had my last ever walk with my big beastie bestie Theordore. He was loving life, having the greatest morning.It was his favourite kind of day - we'd gone for our quick car trip to take Daddy off to the airport and I decided Theo and I would go watch the sunrise at the beach. He was having a fabulous time, sniffing, and marking every tree he came across, playing with a random doggy friend on the beach and prancing around as if he owned his surroundings, his beautiful tail held high and his loveable goofy face as proud as punch. But that all changed ever so quickly and dramatically when in a split-second Theo collapsed on the sand, and I sat with him as he breathed his last breath.

As you can imagine, I went into a bit of shock and I was so very sad. I also had a significant problem on my hands. It was just Theodore and I currently on the beach. He was as big as me. I had no idea what to do. I couldn't even think straight. My prayer went something like "God you seriously need to help me here, I don't know what to do". I sat for a bit with Theodore and wondered who to ring. I tried my vet emergency number, but they were unable to help, and they gave me another number who didn't pick up. All my friends lived on the other side of town; plus, it was a school and work day. I couldn't think of who to call. Then I looked up and noticed a lady had walked onto the beach with her dog. As I was aware the sight of Theo passed away could be quite confronting for people going for their early morning walk, I decided to leave Theo's side and walk towards her. I was crying when I reached her. "I'm really sorry for bombarding you first thing in the morning, but my dog has just collapsed and passed away on the beach, I'm really sad and can't think straight.Do you know who I could call to come help me as I have just dropped my husband to the airport and can't think of what to do".

This beautiful stranger teared up herself and said that she was so sorry. She went to her car and got a blanket so we could cover him up while we considered what to do. I won't go into all the conversations that took place, but here is the end result of what unfolded that morning. That wonderful lady went and picked up her husband to come and help, and while she did that another beautiful soul sat with me, waited and connected with me. The lady and her husband arrived back to the beach with a plan of attack and after greeting me, they laid out their idea, which was to put Theo on top of the blanket, and we would all lift corners and drag/carry him off the beach to my car. I was so grateful to this beautiful couple and agreed their plan could work!

As I bent down to pick up my corner of the blanket, I absolutely lost it. I sobbed my heart out. The lady who had been sitting with me scooped me into her arms and just held me. I'd never been held by, nor received such comfort or strength from a stranger before. It was so special and just what I needed at that moment. After I had calmed down, I looked to see where the couple and my Theo were. They had already managed to drag him halfway along the beach on their own. What amazing people! I had a small chuckle at Theodore having a ride along the beach and we quickly caught up and grabbed our corners. Another lady walked up and offered her help and grabbed onto the blanket. Five people working together. We eventually got back to the car park where another gentleman got out of his car and joined in, helping significantly to lift Theodore into my car.

It was a mammoth task, one that no person there envisioned needing to complete early that morning – yet these incredible humans came to my aid both physically and emotionally. They warmed my heart that morning, connecting with me through their words, their actions, and their eyes and I was able to see so much beauty on such a sad morning. I cannot thank them enough for what they did for me, my Theodore and in fact my family.

Since this all took place, I can't help but have a thankful heart. Firstly, for the amazing people on the beach that morning. The way in which they supported me will forever be etched in my heart. Secondly, I am thankful for the life of Theodore. Even though Theodore's life was way too short, and I and my family are going to miss him tremendously, I have realised that Theodore lived life ever so well, right up until the end. He had run through the puddles, rolled in the mud, and had played hard with both his doggy and human friends. He had absolutely loved the beach and he was fiercely loyal to his family, keeping his ever-protective eyes on us all – which was particularly difficult when all of us would go for a walk to the beach together! Poor Theo trying to keep us all safe and together!

Theodore had no idea how many days he had ahead of him; none of us did. We'd hoped for a few more years, but his heart had other plans. Theo lived well, he had loved his people and life in general, and found joy in the simplest of pleasures. And that is exactly how I want to live my life. I want to jump in the puddles (probably not roll in the mud!), be fiercely loyal to my tribe, and embrace all that life has for me, finding the joy in the seemingly ordinary everyday.

How about you?

My encouragement today: Theodore taught me so much. He brought so much love and laughter to our family. I hope my short stories and small insights have blessed you in some way, I hope they have encouraged you to see the joy in the world around you, to embrace life, to go after your dreams and to be both brave and strong in all that you do, with all that is in your hands.

* * *

Going deeper....

What impacted your heart from today's story?

What insights have you gained over the course of reading through these stories and reflections?

Do you plan to implement any changes into your every day?

Moving forward, how will you embrace life more fully?

Embrace Your Life - Now it's Your turn!

"Gratitude makes sense of our past, brings peace for today, and creates vision for tomorrow."
Melody Beattie

When I started journalling my thoughts from my life with Theodore, I thought I would have many more stories to come. I hoped for a few more years of sharing life with our big Theodore. There were no signs to indicate we were towards the end of his life, but this is where Theodore's story ends. I'm sure while I'm reminiscing plenty more stories will come to mind and I could create meaning from them, but that is not the purpose of this journal. This journey for me is about learning from my life with Theodore and sharing these lessons with my family and friends. It's about actively seeking to see the beauty and to see the lessons that are all around me. My desire is to be the best version of me so that I can be the wife, mum, daughter, and friend that I long to be for those around me and to really embrace the life that I have been given.

So now it's your turn. If you long to embrace all that life has for you, then I challenge you to go in search of the beauty and the lessons that are all around you. You'll find these lessons while out in nature, within your family interactions, in the workplace; literally anywhere you look or place your feet. And if you don't know how to begin, I encourage you to begin to see the beauty that is in your world and write about who or what you are deeply thankful for. Having a thankful heart turns our eyes towards what truly matters, it helps us to have clarity, and brings a new perspective. It is when we are truly thankful that we can begin to live our life on purpose, living the life we've only ever dreamt of.

Thank you for joining me on this journey. I pray that you have been reminded of the beauty of life, of the joy that is within it, and that you are not only feeling encouraged but, more than that, you have been challenged to take hold of all that life has for you.

Much love

Aly x

PS. Check out the final Chapter of this book where you will find some gratitude journal ideas just to get you started – enjoy!

Next Steps

If you have enjoyed these stories and challenges and would like to connect with me further, there are a few options:

- Firstly, I would love to hear from you! Send me an email at aly@bbravebstrong.com and me how this book has impacted you personally.

- Next, let's begin your coaching journey. Diving deep into the questions posed within this book with a coach can result in powerful outcomes in your life. I would be honoured to join you on your journey. Our initial conversation will be completely free with absolutely no pressure for further coaching. As per all coaching conversations our chat will be confidential, judgement free and a safe space to explore whatever is on your heart - I can't wait to hear from you!

· Not quite ready to begin coaching? That is fine! Why not tune into my podcast 'Brave, Strong and Fulfilled - real life with Kath and Aly'. New episodes go live every Thursday and can be listened to via most streaming platforms.

· Ensure you connect with me on social media so you can continue to receive regular encouragement and sign up for my weekly newsletter.

· And lastly, check out my website https://bbravebstrong.com/ - Here you'll find further resources, including short courses to support you on your journey.

Don't be shy! Reach out, I look forward to connecting with you.

21 Day Gratitude Journal

Day 1 – Write down 3 things you are thankful for today and why.

Day 2 – Take a moment to appreciate something in nature, it could be a beautiful sunset or gorgeous flower. Describe what you see, how it makes you feel, what it causes you to think about.

Day 3 – Write about a moment or time that made you feel truly blessed.

Day 4 – Think about someone who has been there for you through thick and thin. Make a note about how they have positively impacted your life.

Day 5 – Write about a time when someone showed you kindness and how it impacted you.

Day 6 – Think about a challenge or obstacle that you can now be grateful for because it taught you something important – write it down.

Day 7 – Reflect over your life and write about a mentor who has positively impacted you and how you are grateful for their influence.

Day 8 – Make a list of five things that bring you joy and happiness.

Day 9 – Write about a place you are grateful for, whether it be your home, a favourite vacation spot, or a cozy coffee shop.

Day 10 – Make a list of five things you are looking forward to in the future and why you are grateful for them.

Day 11 – Take a moment to appreciate your community and write about something you value in regards to it.

Day 12 – Think about and write down three things that make you laugh or smile.

Day 13 – Take a moment to appreciate your body and list three things you are thankful for.

Day 14 – Call or text someone you appreciate and let them know why you are grateful for them.

Day 15 – Make a list of ten things you are grateful for right now.

Day 16 – Take a moment to appreciate your job or career and write about how it has positively impacted your life.

Day 17 – Write about a pet or animal you are grateful for and how they bring joy to your life.

Day 18 – Is there a particular food or meal you are grateful for? Write about why it brings you joy.

Day 19 - Take a moment to consider and appreciate your senses (sight, smell, taste, touch, and hearing) and write about three things you are noticing with each sense.

Day 20 - Make a list of three things you are proud of and grateful for in regards to your personal growth or development.

Day 21 - Make note of any changes you have noticed after completing these 21 days of gratitude. Write how this experience has encouraged you both in regards to your current season and for your future.

About the Author

I am a wife, a mum of 5 incredible young adults and teenagers plus a daughter-in-love, a daughter, sister, aunty and friend! I have had the honour to work as both a primary and high school teacher, along with working as a Careers Advisor. I absolutely love the outdoors, I love pottering in my garden, hiking and running and I have had the opportunity to run a variety of road and trail marathons. I also love to renovate, having completely renovated our last two family homes. And here's what I have discovered about myself through all of these experiences... I love growth and I love people! I especially love encouraging people to be all that they have been created to be as they navigate life's hurdles. That is why I have started my own business Bbrave Bstrong, completed my studies as a Practitioner in Neurocoaching and currently work as a Life Coach.

You can connect with me on:

🌐 https://bbravebstrong.com

📘 https://www.facebook.com/BbraveBstrong

🔗 https://linktr.ee/alylayt

Printed in Great Britain
by Amazon